I am a Hippo

Written By
Linda Bygrave

Illustrated by
Andy Cooke

Chrysalis Children's Books

I am a hippopotamus.

My name is very big – and so am I!

You can call me hippo for short.

I live in rivers, in Africa.
I am amphibious, which means
that I live in water and on land.

I am as big as a car, and much heavier.
I have a very thick skin, but not much hair.
Can you see my hair?

I can open my huge mouth very wide.

My jaws and teeth are very strong.

I could bite a crocodile in half!

I am a very good swimmer.
I can also walk on the river bottom
and hold my breath for five minutes.

My eyes, ears and nostrils are on top of my head. I can swim through the water with only the top of my head showing.

Over there is a pygmy hippo.
She's much smaller than I am
and lives in jungles.

She doesn't spend as much time
in the water as I do.
Anyway, this book is about ME!

My skin dries out quickly in the hot sun.
I sweat a pink sticky oil to help keep it moist.

In hot weather, I love to cool down
by wallowing in muddy pools.

I do most of my eating at night.
Grass is my favourite food.

I leave the water in the evening and follow
a special trail to a patch of grass I like.

I follow the same trail back
to the water in the morning.
I mark my trail with piles of dung.

I spend the day lazing in the water,
or basking in the sun, with my friends.

I am a mummy hippo.

I live in a herd with other mummy hippos.

Here is a daddy hippo.
We meet to make a baby.

I only have one baby at a time.
I leave the herd when my baby
is ready to be born.

My baby can walk and swim
soon after he is born,
but he can't hold his breath like I can.

He likes to ride on my back
if the water is very deep.

My baby drinks my milk
to make him big and strong.

Soon, we join the herd of other
mummies and babies.

I sometimes look after other hippos' babies, too. I make them walk behind me in a line.

We are off for a wonderful wallow in the mud now. Goodbye!